Loving
Without Fear

Love is a fruit in season at all times,
and within reach of every hand.

Mother Teresa

Balboa Press books may be ordered through booksellers or by contacting:

Balboa Press
A Division of Hay House
1663 Liberty Drive
Bloomington, IN 47403
www.balboapress.com
1-(877) 407-4847

BAL
PRES
A DIVISION OF HAY H

Loving
Without Fear

L.M. Henders

Any people depicted in stock imagery provided by Thinkstock are models, and such images are being used for illustrative purposes only. Certain stock imagery © Thinkstock.

ISBN: 978-1-45
ISBN: 978-1-452

Printed in the Unite

Balboa Press rev. date:

I dedicate this book to my loving family and
friends, and especially to my late husband
and my mother who encouraged me to write.
Their love and wisdom has inspired me.
The rose on the cover is for you Chuck.

INTRODUCTION

Love

Love is an essence, an atmosphere, which defies analysis as does Life itself. It is that which IS and cannot be explained: it is common to all people, to all animal life, and evident in the response of plants to those who love them. Love reigns supreme over all.

John 13:34,35

Love yourself first, and everything else falls
into line. You really have to love yourself
to get anything done in this world.
Lucille Ball

In their lifetime, some people may experience all the aspects of love and others maybe only a few. It's up to you, you see. As you read this book, open up your hearts, open your eyes and see where this love comes from and where it can go in your life. You'd be surprised what love can do for you. We are made from love. No matter what kind of life you've grown up in, or even if you haven't experienced love in the early years, giving love unconditionally from your heart will open up the world to you. People are drawn to you when you show them courtesy and love, they want to be near you. You radiate love when it's true and meaningful.

The title of this book, "Loving Without Fear," means that there are times when who or what we love leaves us. When you give your heart and love unconditionally, the other person, pet, or plant, will eventually disappear from Earth. But don't let that keep you from loving again, because when it's our time to leave Earth, we carry that love with us, for it never dies. Remember, "It is better to have loved and lost, than to never have loved at all." Truer words have not been spoken.

Love is wonderful, all aspects of it. There are so many different kinds of love and I want to tell you about them. I've experienced just about every kind of love there is. Please join me in this adventure and realize all that love in your heart can be shared so many ways in your life.

One last thought before you embark on this journey. A dear Rabbi friend of mine once told me: "Whenever you feel down and sorrowful in your life, say to yourself quietly, *God is with me, God is with me.* Even if I'm crying and sobbing because of a loss, when I say that to myself the crying stops and I feel so much better. That's love.

CHAPTER ONE

Nothing is more powerful than love,
it's the driving force of "all" things.
L.M.H.

Parental Love

When a baby is born, the first introduction to love is when his or her parents are cooing and doting on this wonderful miracle that God has given them in their lives. Babies respond to this love. They smile, they nestle in your arms and fall asleep feeling safe in your keeping. When they cry because they're hungry or need a diaper change and you take care of this for them, they're content. This is love.

I have a few memories going back to when I was a baby. I remember sitting in a highchair and eating pink pudding! I really do remember this. I loved it. It was raspberry rennet. I was born in 1942 so they didn't have instant puddings then. You had to buy rennet instead. I also remember my mother, Marie, tucking me in at night and during the day when I was in my crib. Happy memories and I felt the love.

I was well protected in my childhood and into my teen years. No matter what happened in my life, even when there were *bumps in the road* as I call them, I was loved. Mother and Dad went through a very tumultuous time in their married life because my Dad, whose name was Phil, was an alcoholic. There were days he wouldn't come home and he lost his job. Even with that, I felt loved. Alcoholism is a disease and it has to be handled as such. The person who drinks has to ask the help of another person if they truly want to stop and change their life for the better.

I'll never forget this night as long as I live. Dad finally realized that he was hitting rock bottom. He had a friend named Ernie who was in AA and Dad asked him for help. This particular night, he was off to his first AA meeting. Dad wanted Mom to go with him but she said, "We have a daughter, I can't just leave her alone." So he went by himself. I heard that conversation and never forgot it. From then on, he went to meetings and realized his addiction and got the help he needed. Oh, once in a while he would "fall off the wagon" and then climb back on again.

I truly believe that if I wasn't in the picture they probably would have divorced. But they both loved me, loved each other, and wanted to make a go of it.

I have always been so proud of him for doing this. It changed all our lives.

My parents wanted another child, and now that my Dad was on the road to recovery from alcoholism, Mom became pregnant. I was a shy and lonely child, so the thought of my Mom giving birth to a boy or girl made me ecstatic. I couldn't wait for the baby to be born. Then in September of 1952 my sister Chris was born. I was so excited about it and loved her so much. I was 10 years older than her and could help Mom feed her and just dote on this new miracle. Life was good. I loved her very much and still do.

A lot of life happened in the following years. We moved from San Francisco to San Mateo and loved living there. Then in 1975, my Dad was diagnosed with pancreatic cancer. He lived the usual six months with it and crossed over in November of that year. I believe that when we love on this earth we take that love with us when we "go Home." Life on the other side is Home. We were sad to see him go from our lives, but in my heart I knew he was just fine where he was. Of course our lives changed from that experience. My family never stopped loving him.

Another aspect of family love are grandparents. I never met my grandfathers, but I had two grandmothers, and loved them both. My paternal grandmother was Lebanese and her name was Anna, and my maternal grandmother was Swedish and her name was Maria. Every summer my Dad would drive us to Sacramento to see his mother Anna. When it was time to eat, the table was laden with food. She spent hours cooking. That was love. She worked so hard in her life it was amazing she had the stamina. My Dad loved her so much and he helped her with anything she needed.

My maternal grandmother, Maria, was a delight. She lived in a home in San Francisco with assisted living. Every Saturday she would come and visit Mother, Chris, and I. She took the bus and walked down the hill to our house on the corner. I waited by the window for her. I couldn't wait to see her. She was funny, caring, and full of love. She always brought me movie magazines. She loved the movies as I did. We would talk about the movie stars and their problems and what movies they were making. I cherished those visits. I miss her so. I felt her love even after she "crossed over." In this book, there are times when I will use the term "crossing over." We are transitioning when we leave this Earth. We are in pure consciousness when we are "Home."

My Mother has a talent for poetry. In closing with family love, I want to share with you this wonderful piece that she wrote from the heart.

Levels of Love

When I was a child I loved trustingly, unquestioningly, without doubt, without fear. My small hand nestled in the palm of Momma's and Daddy's hands as we strolled through the park, and I felt warm and secure because they were near.

As an adolescent I loved in different ways than I loved Mom and Dad, and sometimes my heart would pound, my hands would sweat.

Will he like me? Will he hate me? What can I do or say that will convey to him how thrilled I am that we met?

As a young woman I fell in love, my heart and mind filled with warmth and joy for this man who was soon to be mine forever.

When we were pronounced man and wife, my pulse raced and my heart swelled, for he and I would have an eternal and wonderful life together.

How thrilling to be a mother, to hold this tiny, warm body in my arms, while my love pours out and encompasses and protects this child.

I understand now about the tigers and lions in the jungle and how fiercely the mothers defend their young in the wild.

My daughter is getting married today, and her Dad and I are filled with pride and love that cannot be concealed. She will one day have her own tiny baby to adore and this very special magic from parent to child will one day to her be revealed.

I am a Grandma now, how joyous to once again hear a small voice ask for things.

My love is boundless and I can share so much with them, that after we have all been together, the sheer pleasure of this closeness, this sharing, makes my heart sing.

A child, a youngster, a woman, a bride, a mother, a grandmother, how different each love is from the other and yet so much the same.

Who can say which is the greater, who can say which has the strongest claim?

For now I'm alone, and in love with life with its yesterdays, todays, and tomorrows, pressing, pushing me, involving me, absorbing me until I seek rest.

I reflect at times on how many kinds of love I've known and still know, and silently thank God that I have been so blessed.

CHAPTER TWO

For every person who loves,
there are hearts somewhere to receive it.
L.M.H.

Friends

We all must have friends in our lives. It doesn't matter how many it matters that you have them and cherish them. You need to be a friend to have a friend, and when you love them for who they are unconditionally they will give that love back to you. I've been very fortunate with friends. Most of my closest and dearest friends I have known well over thirty years. We've been through a lot of "life" during our friendships. We've helped each other through our pain, been there to listen to each other when we have something to say or get off our chest, and most of all they have been loyal and trusting. Two very important words. Be true to yourself and to your friends. To quote William Shakespeare:

"This above all: To thine own self be true, and it must follow as the night the day, thou canst not then be false to any man."

I remember years ago, I knew a woman who was very lonely. She alienated her family and didn't have friends. She always wanted to talk to me because she knew I wouldn't judge her and would listen. I felt so bad for her. You have to give love from your heart in order for you to receive it. You can't "look" for love. It has to come from within and there's plenty of it to spread around if only one would do it and open their hearts.

A few of my friends live out of state or many miles away. That doesn't keep us from being friends and to think about each other. We get on the phone periodically and pick up where we left off. We catch up and wish each other happiness and express our love to each other. Thank God for friends and family. They are the source of so much love if we let it happen. I thank God every day for my family and friends and wish them well and to have a safe life. Without them in my life I would be one lonely woman, believe me.

Cherish your friends and give them love freely and never take them for granted. Be there for them, listen to them, and never be jealous of what they have. Never compete with them, for each of us has a road to travel and it may be entirely different from what your friend's road is. I say this with love and years of experience in having and keeping friends.

A quote from Eleanor Roosevelt says it nicely: Friendship with oneself is all-important, because without it one cannot be friends with anyone else in the world.

CHAPTER THREE

Oh what peace lies within when two people
love each other unconditionally.
L.M.H.

Finding the Love of Your Life

I grew up in San Francisco, and as a Freshman in high school I met a fellow at an Ice Skating rink. This place is no longer there because it was torn down years ago. The thing to do on weekends was to go skating and I loved it. A friend of mine in school, Shelley, and I would go there and have a lot of fun. My friend became close to a family friend of mine, James, and he introduced me to Fred. Every weekend we all would go skating. Being on the ice is glorious. When the Winter Olympics come around on TV, I thoroughly enjoy the skating competitions. Fred and I became close and we enjoyed dating.

Approximately two years later my parents, sister, and I moved to the Bay Area Peninsula. This was hard for Fred and I, but he escorted me to my Junior Prom, and the Senior Prom. It was wonderful to have a date for these occasions. The problem was he felt more serious about me than I did about him. That spark of love just wasn't there for me. He was there when I needed a date and that was about it. He was very jealous about everything and very possessive, but it didn't keep me from dating him.

One day my mother, bless her heart (I say that now, but not then), she went on a rampage about Fred and I while we were standing there bewildered. She basically broke us up. Fred left in a huff and I never saw him again. I didn't speak to my mother for two weeks. I was so mad. I was 17 years old and didn't understand why she did this. As I look back, thank God she did.

One evening during this troubled time in my life, I sat down at my desk and wrote Fred a letter saying that we were no longer going to see each other and that was it. Mother found the impression of the note on the pad that I wrote it on and wondered what it was. I informed her that it was good and that I finally broke up with Fred. She was so happy.

Shortly after graduation from high school, I got a job in a bank, and was feeling lonely without a man in my life. Mother encouraged me to go to the neighborhood little theatre and tryout for a play. She said, "Get out of the house and do something." I did. I went to two one-act plays one evening after work and noticed a nice looking man named Chuck who was in one of the plays. He was very handsome. I came home and told my parents about him. I auditioned for the next play which was called, "Warrior's Husband." A wacky and fun "period" piece. Chuck and I were in the play. As fate would have it we talked and talked after rehearsals and performances, and fell in love. Before the play ended 7 weeks later, we were engaged! You never know where love is going to find you.

I went out with Fred for four years but I didn't really know him. I met Chuck and dated him for only a few months and knew he was the one. Our hearts were open and love found its way in. He was the love of my life. Many people in the theatre wondered about this quick romance of ours and weren't sure we were doing the right thing. When it's true love you know it. You feel it with all your heart and soul and there are no doubts.

My point here is, open your heart and let love in. It will surprise you when you least expect it. It brings joy into your life and to those around you. Chuck and I were happy and it showed. People were happy around us and my family was thrilled I found such a wonderful man.

CHAPTER FOUR

Children are the purest form
of love in the universe.
L.M.H.

Children

In April 1961 our daughter Jeannie was born. I became pregnant a month after we were married. I was still learning how to keep house, how to cook, and how to be a good wife! Oh my! It's amazing how quickly we learn those things that are expected of us. We doted on Jeannie and loved having a new precious baby in our lives. Having children is a special kind of love. These amazing human beings are loaned to us from God, to nurture, love, and take care of until they are able to take care of themselves. However, even when they're adults, parents STILL worry about their children for the rest of their lives. Of course there are problems in bringing up children, as there are problems in everything we do in life worth living for. If everything was perfect on Earth, why would we be here? We would be staying on the "other side" rather than coming to Earth and putting up with "bumps in the road". We're here to learn and having children is a learning process as well as a loving process.

Chuck and I went through a rough patch when Jeannie was one year old. Chuck had to have a back operation. His back was in terrible condition and he was in pain all the time. I was also pregnant at the time. I had just found out so I didn't even show yet. I ended up staying at my parent's home for a while because Chuck was in a hospital a good distance from our home. I saw him every day and he came through the operation just fine. In the meantime, I was bleeding and ended up having a miscarriage at my parents house. My parents were out for the evening and I called the house where they were at, and my dad came to get me and drove me to the hospital nearest to my home. Here we were. Chuck and I in hospitals at the same time in opposite ends of the Peninsula. A real bump in the road of life. After a couple of weeks Chuck came home and was off work for three months before going back.

Two and a half years later we had our son Phil. He was born in December 1963. We were experienced parents by this time and knew pretty much what to

do and how to do it. Two and a half yea   a
between our children was wonderful. Je   c
her new brother as we all did. They were   i
wonderful children any parent could ask for.
them both with all of our hearts and were ve
of them.

Today, I see so many troubled children
world. Both parents have to work to make ends
I was very, very lucky because Chuck made en
money in those days that I didn't have to work
of the home. I would be there for our children wh
they got out of school and I was a constant for then
I loved being a mother and staying home cooking and
cleaning. I relished the whole package.

I honestly think that our children stayed out of
major trouble because they knew we loved them
unconditionally. Chuck and I were there for them
always. If they were troubled, we listened. If they hurt
themselves, we patched them up or took them to the
doctor immediately. If they did something wonderful,
we were there complimenting them and giving them
confidence in whatever they did. That's love. I think to
this day that our children are emotionally mature and
able to deal with the problems in their lives because
of that love. If children feel unloved they get into all
kinds of trouble to get attention. They find what they
think is "love" in all the wrong places.

Chuck and I were truly blessed with our children.
We both received love in our lives from our parents

d were able to express that love to our children. If
hildren are abused in their homes growing up, they
n turn abuse their own children. They don't know
how to love because they never received it. It goes on
and on until the pattern is broken. "Oh what a tangled
web we weave!"

Grandchildren

One of the benefits of having children and loving
them is the fact that later in life when they're grown
up and married, they most likely will have children
of their own. More family to love! I adore all six of
my grandchildren with all my heart. My daughter
has a boy and a girl from her previous marriage, and
three step children, two girls and a boy, who are her
husband Dennis' children. My son and his wife Lisa
have three girls and a boy. My grandchildren fill my
heart with joy and wonder. Watching them grow up to
be beautiful people inside and out is awesome. Also,
if I should be so lucky to see it, I look forward to the
day when my grandchildren marry and have children
of their own. That is an added bonus. My mother is
a great grandma and loves it. She's very proud of her
family and so am I.

I have often babysat for my grandchildren and
delighted in it. They were always caring and considerate
and it was a pleasure. It's a closeness I will never forget.
God bless them all.

Years later when Chuck and I were by ourselves after the kids moved out, I quit work and enjoyed staying home with our dogs and doing what I wanted to do when I wanted to do it. It was a very peaceful time in our lives.

CHAPTER FIVE

Love your pets, and cherish them. They are very
close to nature and love unconditionally.

L.M.H.

Pets

Not everyone has the patience and desire to have a
pet. They require care, love, and cleaning up after. It's
a common belief that all animals are close to nature.
They love you unconditionally, and they are loyal and
wonderful to have around. I wasn't able to have a dog
when I was a child, so I lived through and loved the
dogs my friends and neighbors had.

Dogs and cats are also used to cheer up and help
people who are confined in a wheelchair or are in a
care facility. It's wonderful therapy for the patients and
the animals love it. They get the attention they need
and enjoy the friendships that develop with humans.

When I was a teenager and living at home with my parents and sister, we got a wonderful dog named Shelly. She was part Sheltie and something else. Our first dog, and I was so excited. She was a delight and we loved her to pieces. After I broke up with my boyfriend of four years, I was despondent for a while and I would sit on the back stairs and mope. Shelly would come up to me and whine and look forlornly at me and put her paw on me. How sensitive is that? I would then pet her and tell her that everything will be fine and that I'd get over this phase of my life. Pets are very sensitive to our needs and our moods.

Six months after Chuck and I got married, we bought our first home and I was pregnant with our daughter. That's when we got our first dog. We named him Moki. Children and dogs or cats just go together. They need to know how to treat animals and to have the experience of having a pet and caring for them. I'm a dog lover myself. We all have our favorite species to love.

Years later when our kids were grown, I had this notion that I wanted a Great Dane. I picked out our first Dane from a private breeder. The Dane was called Cinnamon. What a wonderful dog. She wasn't treated with a lot of love so it took her awhile to come to us and trust us. I'll never forget the first time she let me pet her.

I was sitting on the back steps going out to the yard. She was standing next to me on my right side. I was talking softly to her and asking her to trust me, and lo and behold she let me touch her and gently pet her. I was thrilled. This happened two weeks after we got her. You can imagine our frustration not being able to get near her. After that, we all could go to her and love her. She turned out to be my very favorite pet of all time. What a lovely, smart, and caring animal she was. Danes don't normally last more than nine or ten years because of their size. All of our Danes lasted for ten or eleven years. They were cared for, loved, and were family.

Later on we moved to a bigger home, and after having a couple more Danes and losing them eventually, we adopted a male and female. They played together and enjoyed each other. During the summer after dinner, the two Danes would stand together looking toward the family room, and wait for Chuck and I to go out and play with them. The male, Duke, would play hide and seek. Mariah, the female, would play tug of war with one of Chuck's old shirts. We really enjoyed this special time with our pets, and they enjoyed it also. They couldn't wait until we came out after dinner each night. Fun times!

The love of a pet fills the heart and I believe God gave us these wonderful animals to do just that. Many people are missing love in their lives and need something to hold, hug, and care for. Pets fill that need.

Pets generally don't last as long as we do. This was Chuck's problem in getting another dog after losing the one we had. After bringing our sick dogs to the vet to be put down he would say, "No more pets." I knew the real reason why. It was too hard for him to lose them. It hurt. But my philosophy was to get another dog and transfer that hurt into loving another pet. You don't stop having pets because you lose them. It hurts, but you go on and love another.

I also have a love of two very special exotic animals in this world. Elephants and giraffes. I adore them. Unfortunately I haven't been up close and personal with either one. I hope to some day. Elephants are so intelligent and have very human emotions when it comes to their loved ones and those that leave this world. They mourn for those they have lost and care for their families with strong bonds. I have a room in my home dedicated to elephants using artifacts and pictures. I also have a room dedicated to giraffes. They're wonderful and charming animals. They're gentle and have the most beautiful eyes of any animal I've ever seen. Of course, I'll never have either one of these animals as pets, but I adore them from afar. Thank God for all the wonderful and beautiful animals we share this earth with. Don't forget how close all animals are to nature. We can learn how to love unconditionally from them.

CHAPTER SIX

This is the luxury of music.
It touches every key of memory and stirs
all the hidden springs of sorrow and of joy.
I love it for what it makes me forget,
And for what it makes me remember.
Unknown Author

Music and Theatre

When I was six years old my parents bought me a brand new piano. I wanted to take piano lessons. It was hard for them to buy it, and they paid for it "on time" for years. I took lessons and practiced and practiced and...You know what I mean if you've ever taken music lessons in your life. When I was even younger than that, I listened to my mother's opera records for hours. I'd lie on the floor and have my ears pressed to the phonograph listening and wishing that I could sing like the professional singers did. I loved opera at a very young age. At that time I didn't realize what my piano lessons and love of classical music would mean in my life later on. It was a necessary thing for me to learn how to play piano for what was to come in the following years.

Music has played a very important part in my life and for my sister as well. When I got married I had to leave my piano at home for a while until my parents could afford to buy Chris a piano. We both practiced and practiced and developed a talent that was good enough to perform in the theatre. My sister went on to earn her Masters Degree in accompaniment and I trained my voice to sing opera. We loved music and still do. It's a love that stirs the soul and helps in any kind of situation in life, good or bad. It's necessary to have music in one's life. It teaches us to love and respect the people who wrote this wonderful music many, many years ago. Of course, there are wonderful composers today who make us feel good and change our mood for the better because of their music.

My husband continued to become a wonderful actor and I pursued my music. As our kids were growing up, we would take turns being in shows so they wouldn't have to have babysitters all the time. As they got older we were able to be in shows together. I sang in a series of Gilbert and Sullivan operettas, had small parts in opera, and then I landed a job in the choir in a Presbyterian church. I consider that the most fulfilling and wonderful singing experience of my life.

I practiced on my voice every day and tried my best at every audition I went to. Sometimes I was lucky and other times I wasn't. That's the way it goes in theatre.

After eight years at the church being the lead soprano soloist, it was time for me to leave and pursue other things. It was a hard decision to make. I loved it there and loved all the singing I was given the opportunity to perform. It was a singer's heaven to have the job that I had. I wouldn't have traded it for anything. Not even for opera and musicals. It was a fulfilling job and I had instant satisfaction with it.

People were moved by our choir's music and with the solos. The choir director made sure he had a lead bass, tenor, alto, and soprano at all times. We never knew how many choir members would show up at the service on Sunday mornings, but he knew that the four leads would be there. This was a paying job and we loved it. What an experience to sing lead in so many beautiful oratorios in that beautiful church in the redwoods. I thank God for the chance to sing in that scenario and to sing for Him.

When the time came for me to leave I was nervous about it. It definitely was the right thing to do, but I was leaving something I loved with all my heart. Nothing stays the same in life. Everything is in constant motion and evolving at a steady pace. It was time and I knew it. It hurt to leave, and it was quite an adjustment.

Years later in our new home, Chuck and I became involved in the theatre in our new town. We were in many plays together and it was wonderful. I so enjoyed being involved in that theater and with Chuck at my side during all the multitude of activities. Theatre was a major part of our life. Many events in our lives were remembered by what plays we were in at the time. A wonderful life with a wonderful man.

CHAPTER SEVEN

Earth has no sorrows that it cannot heal,
Or heaven cannot heal, for the earth is as
Divine as anything the heart of man can conceive.
John Muir

Travel

As the years went by in our marriage, Chuck and I traveled a great deal. We loved the experience and especially loved cruising. We loved the scenery, the people, and the different cultures. It's one of life's pleasures and we enjoyed every minute of it. The first major cruise that we took which included Chuck, Myself, Chris, Mother, Jeannie and Phil, was a gift from my Mother. It was a wonderful trip but it didn't start out without a hitch.

Mother had to have an operation. Afterwards in the healing process, she was experiencing pain. She went to the doctor and it turned out that she had a blood clot in her lung. She was immediately put in the hospital and given blood thinners to dissolve the clot. This came around a short time before we were going to leave on our cruise. She eventually accepted the fact that she probably wouldn't be able to go on this trip. However, I didn't want to accept it. Mother had been on this cruise before and wanted to see our reaction to it. It included Egypt, Israel, Greece, and Turkey.

One day at work, I called her doctor and was lucky to get him on the phone. I said, "Why can't my mother go on this cruise? This is important to her and she's paying for it and wanted to see our reaction to all the wonderful countries we're visiting." He responded with, "Well, she's taking blood thinners and she has been through an ordeal. I don't know if it would be safe for her to go."

I accepted this, and so did Mother. Then one day, Mother went to the doctor for a checkup. When he was done he looked at her and said, "Well, I guess you can go." She said, "Go where?" He said, "On the trip." She was so excited she jumped up and hugged him and immediately walked to our travel agent and told her to stop the presses and don't cancel her ticket. Everything worked out and she was able to go with us. We watched out for her closely on this trip and made sure she didn't overdo anything. It was a memorable and wonderful trip and the first of many cruises we would take.

Here's a message from John Muir: Climb the mountains, and get their good tidings. Nature's peace will flow into you as sunshine flows into trees. The winds will blow their own freshness into you and the storms their energy, while cares will drop off like autumn leaves.

CHAPTER EIGHT

How do I love thee? Let me count the ways.
I love thee to the depth and breadth and height
My soul can reach. I love thee freely,
as men strive for Right;
I love thee purely, as they turn from Praise.
I love thee with the breath, smiles,
tears, of all my life,
And if God choose, I shall but love
thee better after death.
Elizabeth Barrett Browning

Losing Your Significant Other

This probably is the hardest chapter for me to write. It's written with all the love in my soul and my being. In the year 2006, I lost my beloved husband, Chuck, to cancer. This was, as you can imagine, a very major change in our lives. I also know that a lot of you out there have experienced this kind of loss in your life. It's always hard on our hearts to lose anyone we love in our lives. Whether it be a parent, sibling, child, or spouse. It's all hard. What made it more tolerable for me was the fact that I have read "many" books on the subject of death. I have gained an understanding and non-fearful attitude toward those leaving this Earth. In fact, I don't like the word "death." Only our bodies die. They age and deteriorate and we have to leave them eventually. We all do this. It's part of the process of life. We're more alive on the Other Side than we can imagine. What makes it hard for us when someone we love leaves, is the fact that we can't talk to them and receive a response or feel them physically anymore. We won't see them walking around or coming in the door.

Chuck went to the doctor for a physical and was having a little trouble with digestion which was unusual for him. The doctor ordered a CT scan to check out his abdomen. There appeared to be some spots on his liver. As things progressed, the cancer started in the pancreas and quickly invaded the liver. No operation would cure this and he had to have chemotherapy. He had the best doctor available at Stanford Hospital and was started on chemo. They put him on a pill which was experimental but it made him very ill. He was treated with the usual chemo. For seven months he was in pretty good shape with no pain. During the last month it became more severe.

In life, we sometimes are not aware of just what we are capable of when called upon to perform certain tasks for the good of others. I never considered myself to be the nursing type even though I'm very curious and interested in the medical field. But because my love for my husband was immense, I cared for him with all the love in my heart to make him feel comfortable as possible and devoted those months completely to him.

A month before Chuck "crossed over", we went up to Washington to visit our friends and he did very well. It was good that we took the trip. It was the last one we would take together.

When Chuck's health was getting critical, we were in the ER and he was supposed have a room. His liver was in bad shape and he wasn't feeling well at all with this insidious disease. We went to the hospital in early evening and waited in the hallway in ER for his room. We were there until 4:00 am and he still didn't get his room. I went up to the desk and said this man is dying and he needs to be comfortable and needs his room. I was livid. Poor Chuck, he looked at me and said, "Honey, go home, you need your rest." I looked at him and said "I would do anything for you." Finally he got a room after I protested to the nurse at the desk.

On September 25, 2006, my beloved husband crossed over at 8:00 am at home in our bed. It was bittersweet. I was happy that he was relieved of the pain of cancer and at the same time I would miss him terribly. I called the Hospice and they were incredible and helped with everything. We had a contract with Neptune Society for both of us. The next year would prove to be quite interesting. I have it on personal experience my friends, that we don't die. We only leave our bodies and continue on to a wonderful life without pain or worries of any kind. Believe me.

Chuck wanted a celebration of his life at the theatre in town. We had been to several of these celebrations for friends who crossed over. It was wonderful. All our family, friends, and theatre friends were there. Several people got up and said something personal about my husband. I said goodbye to him also. Below is an excerpt of the poem I read, 'I'm Free.' It's beautiful, and my dear lifelong friend who lives in Maui sent it to me to be read at the celebration.

I'm Free

Don't grieve for me, for now I'm free
I'm following the path God laid for me.
I took His hand when I heard his call
I turned my back and left it all.
Author Unknown

What I'm about to tell you is true and I believe it with all my heart. Be comforted by it and know that

you're not alone. When it's our turn to "cross over," we will reunite with our loved ones. Never doubt that.

I had heard that in the first year of losing a loved one, the spirit stays close to us and protects us to make sure that we're doing okay without them. I had "very" vivid dreams of Chuck in that first year. I called them visitations. Very clear, precise, and very loving. I was so in awe of these dreams that I typed a list of them and the dates on my computer. I printed them out so I could read them periodically. They were so comforting and it made me realize even more that we're still very much alive "back Home," and that's wonderful to know.

These visits from Chuck instilled in me the realization that he will always love me, care for me, and be there when I "cross over" someday. In the meantime, I will live my life as full as possible and enjoy life with my family and friends knowing that he is there waiting for me and enjoying "his" life on the other side.

I'd be lying if I said that there aren't moments that I truly miss him and miss his touch. I do cry now and then and at the same time wish him the best and tell him that I'm doing just fine. This is normal. Before I go to sleep each night I talk to him a little, and say how much I love him. I know he's there receiving this message from me and that also gives me comfort.

I want you to know my dear readers, that if love should come into my life again, I won't be fearful of

it. I won't anticipate that I will lose that someone just like I lost Chuck. Always love fully and freely in your life and NEVER fear love in any way or form. Life is full of gains and losses. How we handle it determines the progression of our souls when we reach our goal of "life at Home on the other side."

CHAPTER NINE

No child should die in the dawn of life.
Danny Thomas

St. Jude Children's Research Hospital

When I graduated from high school at seventeen, I broke up with my boy friend of four years and felt lost and lonely. I realized later that I didn't really love him as you should love someone you plan to marry. Yes, I thought I would marry him. My mother could see the disaster of that marriage if it happened, so in her powerful way she stepped in and helped the process of "elimination." I still thank her for this intervention.

During this process of getting used to not have having this man in my life, Mother said to me, "Why don't you pray to St. Jude, the patron saint of *hopeless causes*?" Mother had a dear friend who was a devout Catholic and she bought me a statue of St. Jude. I did pray and I kept the statue in my bedroom. I didn't know much about this very special saint, but lo and behold after only a couple of months, I met my lifetime partner.

To this day, I don't know what happened to the statue, but St. Jude is once again in my life in a very different capacity.

A couple of years ago I received in the mail, an invitation to donate money to St. Jude Children's Research Hospital. Mind you, I had forgotten about praying to St. Jude in my teens at this point in my life. I donated to St. Jude and then the following month I received another request for more money. I sent another check. Now, I send them money every month.

I had the profound privilege to visit the Hospital last year and attend an extraordinary symposium about their research and where it's going. Magnificent! The majority of the children there have a remarkable recovery rate. When you're there you can't help but love the place and the children, and everyone who works there. It's a place of love. You don't feel like you're walking through a hospital at all. Artwork fills the walls of this special place and there's love all around.

When you look into the faces of the children , the nurses, parents, and doctors, what you see are smiles and hope. One can't help but feel uplifted by this.

Deep inside their hearts, the caretakers love their patients and you can see it in their faces and by their actions.

What an amazing place St. Jude Hospital is. The research team is truly one of the world's best. I believe they love what they do and are thrilled when they come up with a medication or cure for many of the diseases these children are sick with.

Danny Thomas' prayers were answered many years ago and the hospital is the result of this prayer. God bless all of them who work there and care for these children. I plan to go there as often as I can. I have love in my heart for these children and being able to donate to them on a regular basis is something I'm very thankful for.

CHAPTER TEN

When you like yourself and then
learn to love yourself,
you are ready to share that love
with all living things.
L.M.H.

Liking and Loving Yourself

One of the many important things I've learned in life is that you must like yourself first then love yourself before you can share that love with anyone or anything else. It starts with you and only you. We are much too hard on ourselves. If we don't do something right, we punish ourselves. If we say the wrong thing, we reprimand ourselves. We are "all" in this together. Every human being on this earth is connected in some way. We are all part of a vast loving energy and light that we call God, and He loves us no matter what we do and say in our lifetime. If He doesn't punish and berate us, why do we have to do it? Think about it. We are "not" perfect by any means. The only thing perfect that exists when life is finished on this earth, is "Home".

We learn from our mistakes, believe me. That's why we make them. It upsets me when I see someone yelling at another person when they've done something wrong or if they weren't thinking clearly when they did it. The person who is yelling, has also done something wrong in his or her life. The right thing to do is show that person who erred how to do it properly.

Please love yourself and realize what a unique being you really are. Every one of us has talents and creativity inside. All we need to do is sit quietly and not think of negative things and let your mind go and look for these talents in a meditative state. Ask for help from God if you can't realize what your talents are. It could be anything that you create from your very own mind. When you find this talent, nurture it, love it, and make it a big part of your life.

Never feel intimidated when someone has talents that you don't have. They aren't any better than you are. They are just different. The world needs all kinds of talent and creativity and benefits from all of it. When you create and develop your talents it opens the door to loving yourself and realizing that you are indeed unique and have something to offer. You're special. Don't forget it.

Don't listen to people who yell at you and say you're useless, or you goofed, or you're worthless. Those poor people are the ones who don't like or love themselves. They haven't learned how to do this. I will say that some people have grown up in an environment that wasn't loving. Their parents didn't show them the love they deserved. What you must not do is use that as an excuse for not having love in your life. Break this tendency to not show or realize love by saying, "I'm talented, I have a loving heart, and there is much beauty around me to love, and I came from love, and I'm okay and have confidence in myself." Repeat this often and you'll soon realize that it helps and makes sense to you.

Just live life with love in your heart, and be kind to everyone around you no matter what mood they're in. With this positive feeling coming from you, you'll soon realize how wonderful life can be. Everything looks better for you, and yes, there will be bumps in the road of life, but that's to be expected. It's how you handle them that counts. Not with negativity, hate, or malice, but with an idea of how to smooth that bump. We all have them. There's no doubt about it. We learn from these setbacks and we learn to have a respect for ourselves when we change what needs to be changed and notice how much better things are.

Love yourself, have confidence, and be happy you are here to contribute to this world we live in. Yes, you do contribute no matter what it is. Having a loving heart for people and other living things is a major contribution.

CHAPTER ELEVEN

Everybody wants to love and be loved. Open your
hearts and love will flow into you. He who has love
is rich, he who doesn't have love has nothing.
L.M.H.

The Love of Giving

Always give with an open heart. Greed is not rewarding
and leaves one feeling unloved and troubled. Always
give with no strings and no reservations. There's a joy
in giving. My Mother was the most generous person
on this earth. Mother "always" gave her love and
support no matter what.

Some people give with strings attached. In other
words, I gave to you, now it's your turn. How wrong to
feel that way. It makes the recipient of this "gift" feel
obligated. You need to give with an open hand and
heart. More important than material things is to give

love and support and you'll feel just as wonderful. The recipient will also feel the love and that's more than any material thing could do. Giving of one's time, heart, and love, is the most generous thing you can do.

Maybe you have a favorite charity. Give to them for they certainly could use it. Maybe someone you know is feeling upset and hurting. Give your love and support and watch the smile on that person's face. Do you love animals? Go to the animal shelters and look at the sad and lonely faces of those creatures, and take one home. See the change in that pet immediately. It feels loved, wanted, and cared for. That's giving. Never give with the thought that you're losing something, or giving something away with nothing in return. The return is seeing how happy you make people and also those lonely animals at the shelter. When they're happy, so are you.

A loving and giving heart is a precious thing. Not everyone has the desire to do this but everyone has the capability to do it. Never say "What's in it for me!" Make someone happy, make an animal happy. Even make a plant happy. They're alive and I believe in their own way they feel. There's a saying to "give until it hurts". But I guarantee you when you give all you can give it won't hurt. It'll make you feel useful, happy, and grateful to be able to make someone happy and improve their lives.

CHAPTER TWELVE

A mother's love is nurturing,
passionate, unconditional,
and the most forgiving in all of nature.
L.M.H.

A Mother's Love

This chapter was not planned. It came about recently because my beloved mother crossed over on May 7, 2010. She was only sick for five weeks and decided at 88 years of age that she was ready to go "Home". If she had lived, she would have been wheelchair bound and in a rest home. This she definitely didn't want. She had strokes which incapacitated her and she had a strong enough will and spirit to leave us right then and there. God bless her. We all should be so lucky to know when we need to leave.

When someone you love leaves to go "Home", you think of all the wonderful times you had together, all the trips, all the things that meant so much. They seem to mean more to us later in life when we lose that special person. The past few years Mom would cook for Chris and I on Sunday nights. Bless her heart. In her eighties and she was cooking for us each week. I miss that terribly. I miss our talks about the world about the "Home" we go to when we leave this earth. It all happened too quickly for us but it was a blessing for her she didn't suffer and she was able to leave quickly for her new life.

Mother was a very generous person. She gave of herself freely and listened to anyone who needed to tell her their troubles or wanted to share something in their lives. She listened and gave advice from her heart never expecting anything in return. That's giving! She loved her family passionately and showed it, and would defend those she loved with her life.

Weeks before Mother crossed over, she was saying that she realized she was a catalyst in this life and felt that was her purpose. She encouraged my sister and me with music lessons which led us to perform later in life and was supportive and gave us the opportunity. Mother was the one who encouraged me to go to Hillbarn Theater where I met my wonderful future husband. She was the one who suggested we have a white Christmas one year, and the whole family went up to Twain Harte and rented a cabin and woke up in the morning with snow outside. Mother convinced me to meditate through Transcendental Meditation. Thirty five years later I'm still meditating. She also treated the whole family to a major trip to the Middle East as I mentioned in an earlier chapter. It was a cruise and it started the whole trend of cruising for Chuck, Chris, Mother, and I in the future. The list goes on and on.

Yes, Mother was a catalyst. I talk to her even though she's gone and ask her to keep on being the catalyst and push me in the right direction that I need to go. This book is dedicated to her and I will always and forever love her with all my heart. I was so privileged to have her as a mother in this life.

This was a woman who loved without fear.

ACKNOWLEDGEMENTS

I would like to thank my wonderful family and friends for their encouragement and love, because without it, this book couldn't have been written.

Thank you Jessica Swanson, my granddaughter, for your wonderful artwork which enhances this book beautifully. I felt your love in every picture and I love you for it.

I also want to thank my family and loved ones who have gone "Home." Your encouragement and love lifted my soul in the writing of this book.